THE TRIAL OF OSCAR WILDE

PENGUIN

PENGUIN BOOKS

Published by the Penguin Group. Penguin Books Ltd, 27 Wrights Lane, London W8 5TZ, England. Penguin Books USA Inc., 375 Hudson Street, New York, New York 10014, USA. Penguin Books Australia Ltd, Ringwood, Victoria, Australia. Penguin Books Canada Ltd, 10 Alcorn Avenue, Toronto, Ontario, Canada M4V 3B2. Penguin Books (NZ) Ltd, 182–190 Wairau Road, Auckland 10, New Zealand · Penguin Books Ltd, Registered Offices: Harmondsworth, Middlesex, England · This extract is from *Oscar Wilde*, by Richard Ellmann, first published by Hamish Hamilton 1987. Published in Penguin Books 1988. This edition published 1996. · Typeset by Rowland Phototypesetting Ltd, Bury St Edmunds, Suffolk. Printed in England by Clays Ltd, St Ives plc
10 9 8 7 6 5 4 3 2 1

'I Am the Prosecutor in This Case'

It often happens that the real tragedies of life occur in such an inarticulate manner that they hurt one by their crude violence, their absolute incoherence, their absurd want of meaning, their entire lack of style.

MOUNTING PRESSURE

'All trials are trials for one's life,' Wilde would declare after his trials were over and his destruction by them was complete. Still, it was a paradox after his own manner that the first trial should not be his own but the one he forced upon Queensberry, whose life was in no such jeopardy. John Sholto Douglas, the ninth Marquess, was a very rich man. He could have lost a dozen libel cases without flinching, and no doubt would have persisted in hounding Wilde whatever happened in court. This was so plain that Wilde's litigiousness gave proof of a distraught mind rather than an indignant one. The trial ended the two years of provocation. From Queensberry's point of view, of course, he was the victim not the aggressor. Wilde and Douglas had tauntingly continued to appear with each other in spite of his repeated threats to go to Scotland Yard. From Wilde's point of view, it was intolerable that a boor and bully should dictate his conduct. Moreover, his life with Douglas, including the publicity of their romantic passion, reflected his intention to oblige a hypocritical age to take him as he was.

Verbal abuse was something to which Wilde was accustomed, and few of the attacks he had suffered during his forty years had drawn blood. He had weathered the mockery of the American and British press over his aesthetic renaissance. Once Whistler had accused him of the purely literary crime of plagiarism, but he had outlived the charge and vindicated himself as an original genius. Much of the gossip about his homosexual tendencies had disappeared with his marriage, but, courting disfavor as he was prone to do, he had roused more gossip by *The Picture of Dorian Gray* and 'The Portrait of Mr W.H.' Even Lillie Langtry talked against him at this time. There had been literary attacks upon him in 1881, from *The Colonel* and *Patience*; 1892, from *The Poet and the Puppets*; and 1894, from *The Green Carnation*. If he was accused of being precious, plumed and effeminate, he had checked his accusers by intellect and grace. After all, even Queensberry had submitted for an hour or two to his charm.

Wilde seems to have overlooked his vulnerability. He was confident of the devotion of his many friends in the political and literary world. With some of them he did not trouble to be circumspect. So he said to the actress Aimée Lowther, 'Aimée, if you were only a boy I could adore you.' Ellen Terry said innocently, 'Oscar, you really didn't mean it?' An embarrassed silence fell, and Henry Irving had to explain to her later. His attitude to sexual transactions was the conventional one of his class. He did not think of his behavior with boys as of any consequence. Except for Shelley, they were prostitutes, to be bought or sold. The boys knew Wilde had treated them well, but tried to make him treat them better still. As for Douglas, Wilde had a right to feel virtuous rather than not. Having long since given up sexual relations with him, he might think of their attachment as an approximation of the Greek ideal. Wilde had made some effort to check Douglas's excesses, and had rescued him from a number of scrapes. If anyone had ruined Bosie, in Wilde's view, it was his parents. Queensberry had treated Bosie even in infancy with contempt for his physical weakness, and Lady Queensberry, in reaction to the paternal bullying, had spoiled him. Queensberry was unruly though he loved rules.

That Wilde anticipated the result of his actions is unlikely, though his sense of doom had been present since childhood. He believed in his unlucky star as much as in his lucky one. The exfoliation of his nature licensed recklessness and promoted foreboding. His first success, 'Ravenna', had described a city fallen from greatness. That he might lose 'a soul's inheritance' is foreshadowed in his prefatory poem, 'Hélas!' Tragic themes had come to him earlier than comic ones. For a man who condemned sacrifice, his plays were full of it. Vera dies to save the Czar, Guido attempts to die to save the Duchess only to have her die as well. Mrs Erlynne sacrifices herself for her daughter as Mrs Arbuthnot has sacrificed herself for her son. The Happy Prince sacrifices himself to help the poor: sacrifice is close to suicide. In *Dorian Gray* both the hero and Sibyl Vane kill themselves, though Dorian does it with more ambiguity. Wilde needed less Greek than he had to know that overreaching would attract Nemesis.

 His prosecution of Queensberry for criminal libel

was the end not the beginning of a long series of legal maneuvers. He had consulted Humphreys about a prosecution in May 1894 and again in July. Queensberry had also taken advice. In the summer of 1894 some passionate letters of Wilde to his son fell into his hands, in particular the Hyacinth letter (either the original or a copy), and a letter of March 1893 which said, 'You are the divine thing I want, the thing of grace and beauty.' Wilde had bought back others, but not these. Queensberry's solicitor advised that the letters alone would not sustain a charge of sodomy against Wilde, so he had adopted the allegation that Wilde was a posing sodomite, which did not necessarily entail commission of the offense. His plea of privilege as a father could be invoked. If Queensberry was not a father in feeling, he was one in fact, and fully exploited this role. His blood was up and he was determined to make Wilde pay for what he appeared to be doing. He would protect his son from similar charges by his influence with the authorities. Queensberry's memories of the death of his son and heir, and of the nullification of his marriage, were still fresh. By bringing down an established reputation like Wilde's he could remake his own, as Prince Hal said he would do by conquering Hotspur.

Wilde and Douglas talked over the situation during the weeks that followed their separate returns from Algiers. Up to now they had told the other members of the family, including Bosie's brother Percy (Lord Douglas of Hawick), now the eldest son, that Queensberry was a victim of delusions. Wilde urged Douglas to tell his brother the truth, but Douglas, though reckless, was not brave, and refused. He proposed to go on just as in the past. By now Wilde was living entirely away from home. On 28 January Constance had to approach Ross to ask Wilde for some money for her when he came home from Algiers, as she was going to Torquay for a month. On 12 March she still did not know her husband's address. Three days later she thanked Ross for sending it. The reason for her ignorance of his whereabouts was that he was avoiding her.

During this time he took rooms at the Avondale Hotel in Piccadilly. Douglas came to stay with him, and ran up a lavish bill at once. Wilde was distinctly uneasy. Queensberry had been denied entrance to the opening night of *The Importance of Being Earnest*, and forced to content himself with leaving a bouquet of vegetables at the stage door instead of making the public denunciation which he had planned. Humphreys, consulted again, wrote on 28 February that he could do nothing because neither Alexander nor his staff would give evidence. When Douglas proposed to keep a young man in the hotel at Wilde's expense, Wilde refused. Douglas left the Avondale in a pet, and moved to another hotel with the friend. There followed a series of letters accusing Wilde of cowardice.

THE BOOBY TRAP

In your war of hate with your father I was at once shield and weapon to each of you.

[illegible]tters came on Thursday morning, 28 [illegible]efore Wilde set out for the Albemarle [illegible]m his hotel. The club was to prove [illegible]e father any more than the hotel had [illegible]from the son. The hall porter, Sidney [illegible]ately handed him the card left by the [illegible]eensberry ten days before. Wright had [illegible]the words – no one was to do so accur- [illegible]nderstood that an insult was intended an[illegible] on the back the details of its receipt, 4.30 on 1[illegible]bruary. Wilde probably made out the words as 'To Oscar Wilde, ponce and Somdomite'. He did not smile at Queensberry's aristocratic misspelling, but took it as a written and public repetition of the charge Queensberry had made in Tite Street. What Queensberry actually wrote was 'To Oscar Wilde posing Somdomite', but in court he said that the words were 'posing as a Somdomite', an easier accusation to defend. What he had wanted, from leaving the card, was an interview. Wilde was goaded beyond that.

For Wilde the significance of the card was that Queensberry, having failed to invade his theatre, was invading his club. There was no hope of confining the matter to private correspondence, or to the knowledge of a small circle. Understandably Wilde felt sorry for himself, on receiving from the father a message as vitriolic as that he had received an hour earlier from the son. 'I felt I stood between Caliban and Sporus,' he wrote to Alfred Douglas later. He went back to the hotel with the idea of bolting to Paris, as he had once before. But the manager, hearing of his intention, said that he must first pay his bill, and that until he did his luggage would be impounded. Wilde did not have the money, and felt trapped.

He was more vexed than despairing. Queensberry must be stopped from making these wanton attacks.

He wrote to Douglas asking him to call early on Friday morning, but to Robert Ross he wrote more fully:

Dearest Bobbie, Since I saw you something has happened. Bosie's father has left a card at my club with hideous words on it. I don't see anything now but a criminal prosecution. My whole life seems ruined by this man. The tower of ivory is assailed by the foul thing. On the sand is my life spilt. I don't know what to do. If you could come here at 11.30 please do so tonight. I mar your life by trespassing ever on your love and kindness. I have asked Bosie to come tomorrow.

Ever yours
Oscar

He wrote to George Lewis to ask his advice, but Lewis reminded him that he had already been engaged by Queensberry. Afterwards Lewis was to say that, if he had been free to advise Wilde, he would have told him to tear up Queensberry's card and forget about it.

When Ross came round that night, he urged Wilde to take no action, but when Wilde persisted suggested he consult Humphreys again. Wilde agreed, and in the morning took Douglas with him to the solicitor's chambers. Douglas was triumphant: his father had put down his charge in writing and could now be prosecuted. Before his friend's eagerness Wilde began to have doubts, but there was no resisting Douglas's fierceness. ‘It is what we fear that happens to us,’ he said. Humphreys displayed a combination of opportunism and naïveté. He scented a spectacular case, saw a celebrity eager to take on another celebrity in court, and urged prosecution. He cannot easily be absolved of blame, since he must have known that Ross, who had sent Wilde to him, was homosexual, and he had the evidence of great intimacy between Douglas and Wilde before him. He chose to suspect nothing, though he asked the routine questions and received decorous answers. As Wilde afterwards remarked, ‘What is loathsome to me is the memory of interminable visits paid by me to the solicitor Humphreys in your company, when in the ghastly glare of a bleak room you and I would sit with serious faces telling serious lies to a bald man, till I really groaned and yawned with *ennui*.’ Later he would dismiss Humphreys as one ‘who would bluster, and threaten, and lie,’ but the lying was not all on Humphreys’ side. Ross offered to tell the truth to Humphreys and Lord Douglas of Hawick, who was sympathetic: Wilde and Douglas absolutely refused. On the assumption of his client’s innocence, Humphreys announced that a prosecution of Queensberry was bound to succeed. He was a hopeful man. By this time Wilde had lost his initial impetus, and played a last card which he expected to be decisive: he had no money. Bosie, determined to keep him up to the mark, announced that his brother Lord Douglas and Lady Queensberry would be delighted to pay costs. Goaded by the whole Queensberry clan, Wilde had no opportunity to withdraw. Humphreys and Douglas escorted him, a white flower in his buttonhole, to a four-wheeler, which took them to Marlborough Street police station on 1 March. He swore out a warrant for the arrest of Queensberry, which took place shortly afterwards. The Marquess was brought to Marlborough police court on the charge of publishing a libel against Wilde.

To some extent Wilde was the prey of his own consciousness as well as of Queensberry father and son. His inclination to betray himself, such as he attributed to mankind in general in 'Humanitad', was not thoroughgoing. He thought of self-betrayal as proceeding in surges, after which there would be recoveries. The role of victim – Sebastian or Marsyas – was only one among several, including the dandy and the apostle of joy, through which he could see himself passing. In his flirtation with Catholicism, he spoke of going to see Newman 'to burn my fingers a little more.' He half invited obloquy, half lost his nerve in the process, meaning or almost meaning to pull back at the last. But the age in which he lived was unexpectedly eager (like most ages), and the right to choose left him before he had time to exercise it. So he emulated his father's disgrace – also over the implications of a libel suit, exceeded it even, and fulfilled his own half wish to kill the success he loved. It would be wrong to assume that this urge to destroy the beloved object, himself or another, came to him after his fall. In *The Ballad of Reading Gaol* the act of killing what we love is made largely deliberate, as it is also in *Salome*, but in other works Wilde, like Lord Arthur Savile, blamed fate not will. We are by nature our own enemies, 'the lips betraying and the lips betrayed.' We seek the events that unconsciously befit us, which consciously we fear. Flaunting and fleeing, Wilde could not embrace a single course of action.

THE LIBEL SUIT

Blindly I staggered as an ox into the shambles.

The proceedings were launched. Humphreys appeared for Wilde, and Sir George Lewis made his first and only appearance for Queensberry, saying that the Marquess would plead justification. Wilde was asked, 'Are you a dramatist and an author?' He replied airily, 'I believe I am well known in that capacity.' 'Only answer the questions, please,' the magistrate admonished him. It was an untoward beginning. Queensberry, questioned by the magistrate as to whether he had anything to say, replied, 'I have simply, your worship, to say this. I wrote that card simply with the intention of bringing matters to a head, having been unable to meet Mr Wilde otherwise, and to save my son, and I abide by what I wrote.' On this he was committed for trial.

The case was adjourned for eight days. On 7 March Wilde, accompanied by his wife and Douglas, attended *The Importance of Being Earnest*. Mrs Wilde had tears in her eyes. At the hearing on 9 March, Lewis having kept his word and withdrawn from the case out of friendship for Wilde, a barrister appeared instead. This was Edward Carson, a fellow-student of Wilde's from Trinity College, Dublin, and a man of great forensic power. Carson had been admitted to the English bar only a year before, but was beginning to be known. When Wilde learned that it would be Carson against him, he said at first, according to Carson's biographer, 'I'm going to be cross-examined by old Ned

Carson,' as if he now had nothing to fear. But Travers Humphreys, who was C.O. Humphreys' son, remembered Wilde saying to him, 'No doubt he will perform his task with the added bitterness of an old friend.' It was like Isaac Butt with Jane Wilde in the Mary Travers case years before. There is nothing like the courtroom to obliterate fellow-feeling.

Carson, to give him his due, had not entered the case at once. Queensberry's new solicitor, Charles Russell, invited him to accept the brief, but for a while Carson protested that Wilde was a fellow-Irishman from the same university. He had, however, offered another reason when one was enough, the second being that the case against Wilde was too weak. Russell took the hint and set himself to strengthen the case, meanwhile not approaching any other barrister. Help came from an unexpected quarter. Charles Brookfield and Charles Hawtrey, both of whom had profited from Wilde's career by acting in his plays and by writing their parody, *The Poet and the Puppets*, furnished information about his young friends. At the same time private detectives were looking about London, and one, a man named Littlejohn, happened to visit a shop in the West End which the police had under observation. A woman prostitute, asked how business was, said it was very bad because of competition for male clients from boys under the influence of Oscar Wilde. The detective asked eagerly for further information, and was told, 'All you have to do is break into the top flat at 13 Little College Street, and you will find all the evidence you require.' He went there, and pushed past the caretaker, an old woman, who tried to prevent his entry. He had come to the lodgings of Alfred Taylor. In the flat was a kind of post-box, containing the names and addresses of boys with whom Wilde consorted. On this information, he found William Allen and Robert Clibborn, who were hiding in Broadstairs, and soon Wood, Walter Grainger, Alfonso Harold Conway, and others. According to George Ives, these young men were sequestered in a house and terrified into giving evidence against Wilde.

With this new information, and some other leads as well, Russell returned to Carson to ask him to take the brief. Carson deliberated: the details were revolting and abundant enough, and he could see himself triumphant. College loyalty faded before Protestant morality. As a final step he consulted Lord Hailsbury, the previous Lord Chancellor, who urged him to take the case. Finally he agreed. Wilde and Douglas were fairly confident, having no inkling of the new evidence that had been turned up. Douglas was even able to persuade Wilde to take him to Monte Carlo, where, though he said Wilde had cured him of gambling, he gave himself up to the gaming tables, while Wilde sat alone and disquieted. They were away from 13 March for a week or more. An article in the *Observer* said that they were expelled from their hotel in Monte Carlo at the request of other guests. On their return they discussed the case with Humphreys, who advised them to find a reputable witness who would testify that *Dorian Gray* was not an immoral book. Wilde thereupon went, probably on Saturday 23 March, to see Frank Harris. Harris proved himself a true friend: he would give the evidence Wilde wanted. But he asked Wilde about the case, and Wilde explained that Queensberry would not only bring up his formal literary works, but also had got hold of some letters from Wilde to Douglas, in spite of Wilde's effort to pay blackmail and get them back. Harris needed to hear no more. He advised Wilde that the case was sure to go against him even if he were in the right. No jury would convict a father for protecting his son, and the letters would show that Douglas needed protecting. 'You are sure to lose it,' he warned, 'you haven't a dog's chance, and the English despise the beaten – *vae victis!* Don't commit suicide.'

His words frightened Wilde enough to make him agree to meet Harris for a further talk on Sunday night. During the day Harris sampled the opinion of various people, including someone in the office of the Director of Public Prosecutions. The sentiment against Wilde was overwhelming: Queensberry's charges were generally regarded as true. The letters to Douglas and the fact that Wilde had paid blackmail would count heavily. Harris urged that Wilde, as a leading man of letters, had not the right to set the clock back fifty years by rousing full enforcement of the law.

It was agreed to meet again next day at the Café Royal, where Harris had already arranged to have lunch with contributors to the *Saturday Review*, including Bernard Shaw. Wilde asked if he might bring Douglas along, and Harris offered no objection. When he came, however, he was alone. Shaw and Harris were still sitting over their lunch. Shaw offered to leave, but Wilde told him to stay. Wilde asked Harris to testify to the high artistic character of *Dorian Gray*. Harris put the request aside as irrelevant. Instead of answering he now gave an accurate prediction of what was to come. If Wilde would not drop the case, he would certainly lose it. If he dropped it, he could go at once to Paris, and he must take his wife with him.

There could be no staying on in London, since Queensberry would not relent. From Paris he could write to *The Times* in his best style, saying he despaired of receiving justice because Queensberry was pretending to be the good father. After Harris had finished, Shaw registered agreement, and Wilde was swaying that way. Just then Douglas came up to their table. He listened with mounting impatience as Harris reiterated his arguments, and then, as Harris described it, 'cried with his little white venomous, distorted face, "Such advice shows you are no friend of Oscar's."' 'What do you mean?' asked Harris, but Douglas had already turned on his heel to leave the restaurant. To Harris's astonishment, this exit overcame Wilde. He too rose: 'It is not friendly of you Frank, it really is not friendly,' he said. 'Don't be absurd,' cried Harris, but Wilde said, with forced anger, 'No, it is not friendly.' Leonine Wilde sheepishly followed Douglas out.

Wilde had prepared himself to defend his writings, including the letters to Douglas. There was, however, one more legal step. English law requires that the defendant in a libel action must enter his Plea of Justification, with particulars, before the trial begins. This was done by Queensberry on 30 March. Humphreys

 brought Wilde and Douglas to see it on the 1st or 2nd

of April, and they could only find it appalling. In fifteen separate counts, it accused Wilde of soliciting more than twelve boys, of whom ten were named, to commit sodomy:

1. Edward Shelley, between February and May 1892.
2. Sidney Mavor, in October 1892. (Mavor testified that Wilde had done nothing wrong.)
3. Freddie Atkins, on 20 November 1892, in Paris. (His evidence was thrown out.)
4. Maurice Schwabe, on 22 November 1892. (Did not testify.)
5. Certain (unnamed) young men, between 25 January and 5 February 1892, in Paris.
6. Alfred Wood, in January 1893.
7. A certain young man, about 7 March 1893, in the Savoy Hotel.
8. Another young man, on or about 20 March 1893, in the Savoy Hotel.
9. Charles Parker, in March and April 1893.
10. Ernest Scarfe, between October 1893 and April 1894. (Did not testify.)
11. Herbert Tankard, in March 1893 at Savoy Hotel. (Did not testify.)

12. Walter Grainger, in June 1893 in Oxford and in June, July and August at Goring.
13. Alfonso Harold Conway, in August–September 1894 at Worthing and about 27 September in Brighton.

The last two counts spoke of the immorality of *Dorian Gray* and of the maxims Wilde had published in the *Chameleon* in December 1894. These two counts were the ones with which Carson chose to begin.

Although Frank Harris, and other friends, urged Wilde to drop the case, Wilde was constantly being urged by Douglas not to play the coward. 'I can't, I can't,' he told Harris, 'you only distress me by predicting disaster.' Toulouse-Lautrec, in London at the time, found Wilde still outwardly confident and contemptuous of the British public. The strain showed, however, in his tirades and complaints. (He refused to sit for a drawing.) That he accepted the idea of being a martyr may be true, but must be reconciled with his obvious preference for not being one. He was rushed along, by solicitor, lover, barrister, into a situation from which there could be no retreat except voluntary exile, something he detested. Confronted by this choice, better to suffer in Athens than glory in

Thebes. If nothing else, he would put on a good show.

The trial opened on 3 April 1895 at the Old Bailey, before Mr Justice R. Henn Collins. There was the sense that a great legal battle was to be fought, and a crowd watched the arrival of the principals. Wilde drove to court in a brougham with two horses and liveried servants. He entered without smiles. The Marquess of Queensberry, sporting a Cambridge-blue hunting stock instead of a collar and tie, was already in court. Collins arrived ten minutes late, and the trial began. Sir Edward Clarke made the opening speech for the prosecution. He had, as Harris noted, the bleak face and severe side whiskers that went with a nonconformist parson of some time back, but his manner was 'quiet and conversational'. It was not a good performance. Most of it had been composed before he saw the Plea of Justification, and he merely inserted a reference to that at the beginning of his speech. It was no longer simply a matter of injured reputation:

By the plea which the defendant has brought before the Court a much graver issue has been raised. The defendant has said that the statement is true and that it is for the public benefit that the statement was made, and he has given particulars in the plea of matters which he has alleged show that the statement is true in regard to Mr Oscar Wilde. The plea has not been read to you, gentlemen. There is no allegation in the plea that Mr Oscar Wilde has been guilty of the offence of which I have spoken, but there is a series of accusations in it mentioning the names of persons, and it is said with regard to these persons that Mr Wilde solicited them to commit with him the grave offence, and that he has been guilty with each and all of them of indecent practices. It is for those who have taken the responsibility of putting into the plea those serious allegations to satisfy you, gentlemen, if they can, by credible witnesses, or evidence which they think worthy of consideration and entitled to belief, that these allegations are true. I can understand how it is that these statements have been put in the form in which they are found, for these people, who may be called upon to sustain these charges, are people who will necessarily have to admit in cross-examination that they themselves have been guilty of the gravest offences.

The rest was a defence of Wilde's letters to Douglas, which Clarke determined to quote before Carson had a chance to do so, and of his epigrams in the *Chameleon* and his novel *Dorian Gray*. (There was a certain naïveté on Clarke's part in not realizing that he would be dealing with worse stains than those made by ink.) It was an attempt to show that Wilde was orotund but not vicious, that his verbal flowers were not weeds. But the main interest attached to Wilde's testimony.

When he took the stand, he said, 'I am the prosecutor in this case', though it was already clear that by this time matters had been turned round. 'I am thirty-nine years of age,' he said. Carson, a forty-one-year-old Trinity classmate, took note of this computation. The account Wilde now gave of his blackmail by Wood, Allen, and Clibborn was as adroit as it could have been:

WILDE: . . . From November 3rd, 1892, till March, 1894, I did not see the defendant, but in 1893 I heard that some letters which I had addressed to Lord Alfred Douglas had come into the hands of certain persons.

CLARKE: Did anyone say that he had found letters of yours?

WILDE: Yes. A man named Wood saw me at the rooms of Mr Alfred Taylor and told me that he had found some letters in a suit of clothes which Lord Alfred Douglas had been good enough to give him . . .

CLARKE: What happened?

WILDE: When he entered the room, he said, 'I suppose you will think very badly of me.' I replied, 'I hear that you have letters of mine to Lord Alfred Douglas which you certainly ought to have given back.' He handed me three or four letters, and said they had been stolen from him 'the day before yesterday' by a man named Allen, and that he (Wood) had had to employ a detective to get them back. I read the letters, and said that I did not think them of any importance. He said, 'I am very much afraid of staying in London, as this man and other men are threatening me. I want money to go to America.' I asked what better opening as a clerk he could have in America than in England, and he replied that he was anxious to get out of London in order to escape from the man who had taken the letters from him. He made a very strong appeal to me. He said that he could find nothing to do in London. I paid him £15. The letters remained in my hand all the time.

CLARKE: Did some man shortly afterwards come with another letter?

WILDE: A man called and told me that the letter, a copy of which had been sent to Mr Beerbohm Tree, was not in his possession. His name was Allen.

CLARKE: What happened at that interview?

WILDE: I felt that this was the man who wanted money from me. I said, 'I suppose you have come about my beautiful letter to Lord Alfred Douglas. If you had not been so foolish as to send a copy of it to Mr Beerbohm Tree, I would gladly have paid you a very large sum of money for the letter, as I consider it to be a work of art.' He said, 'A very curious construction can be put on that letter.' I said in reply, 'Art is rarely intelligible to the criminal classes.' He said, 'A man has offered me £60 for it.' I said to him, 'If you take my advice you will go to that man and sell my letter to him for £60. I myself have never received so large a sum for any prose work of that length; but I am glad to find that there is someone in England who considers a letter of mine worth £60.' He was somewhat taken aback by my manner, perhaps, and said, 'The man is out of town.' I replied, 'He is sure to come back,' and I advised him to get the £60. He then changed his manner a little, saying that he had not a single penny, and that he had been on many occasions trying to find me. I said that I could not guarantee his cab expenses, but that I would gladly give him half a sovereign. He took the money and went away.

CLARKE: Was anything said about a sonnet?

WILDE: Yes, I said, 'The letter, which is a prose poem, will shortly be published in sonnet form in a delightful magazine, and I will send you a copy of it.'

CLARKE: As a matter of fact, the letter was the basis of a French poem that was published in the *Spirit Lamp*?

WILDE: Yes.

CLARKE: It is signed 'Pierre Louÿs.' Is that the *nom de plume* of a friend of yours?

WILDE: Yes, a young French poet of great distinction, a friend of mine who has lived in England.

CLARKE: Did Allen then go away?

WILDE: Yes, and in about five minutes Clibborn came to the house. I went out to him and said, 'I cannot bother any more about this matter.' He produced the letter out of his pocket, saying, 'Allen has asked me to give it back to you.' I did not take it immediately, but asked: 'Why does Allen give me back this letter?' He said, 'Well, he says that you were kind to him, and that there is no use trying to "rent" you as you only laugh at us.' I took the letter and said, 'I will accept it back, and you can thank Allen from me for all the anxiety he has shown about it.' I looked at the letter, and saw that it was extremely soiled. I said to him, 'I think it is quite unpardonable that better care was not taken of this original manuscript of mine' (Laughter). He said he was very sorry, but it had been in so many hands. I gave him half a sovereign for his trouble, and then said, 'I am afraid you are leading a wonderfully wicked life.' He said, 'There is good and bad in every one of us.' I told him he was a born philosopher, and he then left.

Although Wilde had obviously paid at least £15 blackmail, the episode was too funny to take seriously. In his more heroic mode, Wilde then described the meeting with Lord Queensberry:

WILDE: . . . At the end of June, 1894, there was an interview between Lord Queensberry and myself in my house. He called upon me, not by appointment, about four o'clock in the afternoon, accompanied by a gentleman with whom I was not acquainted. The interview took place in my library. Lord Queensberry was standing by the window. I walked over to the fireplace, and he said to me, 'Sit down.' I said to him, 'I do not allow anyone to talk like that to me in my house or anywhere else. I suppose you have come to apologise for the statements you made about my wife and myself in letters you wrote to your son. I should have the right any day I chose to prosecute you for writing such a letter.' He said, 'The letter was privileged, as it was written to my son.' I said, 'How dare you say such things to me about your son and me?' He said, 'You were both kicked out of the Savoy Hotel at a moment's notice for your disgusting conduct.' I said, 'That is a lie.' He said, 'You have taken furnished rooms for him in Piccadilly.' I said, 'Somebody has been telling you an absurd set of lies about your son and me. I have not done anything of the kind.' He said, 'I hear you were thoroughly well blackmailed for a disgusting letter you wrote to my son.' I said, 'The letter was a beautiful letter, and I never write except for publication.' Then I asked: 'Lord Queensberry, do you seriously accuse your son and me of improper conduct?' He said, 'I do not say that you are it, but you look it' (Laughter).

MR JUSTICE COLLINS: I shall have the court cleared if I hear the slightest disturbance again.

WILDE: (continuing Lord Queensberry's remarks) 'But you look it, and you pose at it, which is just as bad. If I catch you and my son together again in any public restaurant I will thrash you.' I said, 'I do not know what Queensberry rules are, but the Oscar Wilde rule is to shoot at sight.'

I then told Lord Queensberry to leave my house. He said he would not do so. I told him that I would have him put out by the police. He said, 'It is a disgusting scandal.' I said, 'If it be so, you are the author of the scandal, and no one else.' I then went into the hall and pointed him out to my servant. I said, 'This is the Marquess of Queensberry, the most infamous brute in London. You are never to allow him to enter my house again.'

THE CROSS-EXAMINATION

The sins of another were being placed to my account.

Carson rose to cross-examine. His performance has been very much praised. Professionals are impressed by proficiency, and unperturbed by disloyalty. Carson had so much evidence, and of such a kind, that he only needed to be persistent, not clever. Even if he failed to worst Wilde on literary matters, he would impugn the witness's reliability and prepare for unliterary accusations. He began well by forcing Wilde to admit that he was neither thirty-eight years of age, as Sir Edward Clarke had said, nor thirty-nine, as he had said himself, but forty. The purpose of this was not just to catch Wilde out, but also to emphasize the disparity in age between him and Alfred Douglas, who was twenty-four. Carson took up the subject of the *Chameleon*, his questions being intended to suggest that the magazine was a homosexual one. It contained Douglas's poem, 'Two Loves', one heterosexual and one homosexual. 'Did you think that made any improper suggestion?' 'None whatever,' Wilde replied, and called it a beautiful poem. Carson went on to the story, 'The Priest and the Acolyte', and presumed that Wilde had sanctioned the story and approved of its contents. Wilde denied both allegations.

As the cross-examination proceeded, it became clear that Wilde was retorting cavalierly to Carson's questions. Instead of expounding his theory of art as an enhancement and expansion of life, he presented himself as amoral artist and scorned the moral mob. Early in the prosecution case, as Ralph Hodgson recalled, Carson read a passage from *Dorian Gray*, and demanded, 'Did you write that?' Wilde said he had the honor to be the author. Carson laid down the book with a sneer and turned over some papers. Wilde was lost in thought. Presently Carson read aloud a piece of verse from one of Wilde's articles, 'And I suppose you wrote that also, Mr Wilde?' Wilde waited till you could hear a pin drop and then said, very quietly, 'Ah no, Mr Carson, Shakespeare wrote that.' Carson went scarlet. He turned pages again and read another piece of verse and said, 'And I suppose Shakespeare wrote that also, Mr Wilde?' 'Not as you read it, Mr Carson,' Oscar said. The judge said he would clear the court if there was more noise. Wilde deliberately turned his back, folded his arms, and looked far away through the ceiling in rapt concentration. It was effectively done. Carson thundered at him to conduct himself properly: and he appealed to the judge, 'M'lud, M'lud.' Wilde stared deeper into the void for a full minute. Suddenly he swung round as if he heard Carson for the first time and said, assuming a most apologetic tone, 'I beg your pardon, Mr Carson; I do beg your pardon.' When Carson suggested that *Dorian Gray* was perverted, Wilde replied, 'That could only be to brutes and illiterates. The views of Philistines on art are incalculably stupid.' This élitism could scarcely have favored his cause, and Carson drove it home:

CARSON: The affection and love of the artist of Dorian Gray might lead an ordinary individual to believe that it might have a certain tendency?

WILDE: I have no knowledge of the views of ordinary individuals.

CARSON: Have you ever adored a young man madly?

WILDE: No, not madly. I prefer love – that is a higher form.

CARSON: Never mind about that. Let us keep down to the level we are at now.

WILDE: I have never given adoration to anybody except myself. (Loud laughter)

CARSON: I suppose you think that a very smart thing?

WILDE: Not at all.

CARSON: Then you have never had that feeling?

WILDE: No. The whole idea was borrowed from Shakespeare, I regret to say – yes, from Shakespeare's sonnets.

CARSON: I believe you have written an article to show that Shakespeare's sonnets were suggestive of unnatural vice.

WILDE: On the contrary I have written an article to show that they are not. I objected to such a perversion being put upon Shakespeare.

Carson was not capable of cornering Wilde through literary criticism. At last he began on the young men. Wilde had said in direct examination that he denied all the charges in the Plea of Justification which had to do with sodomy. But the mustering of a considerable list by Carson, the multifarious details, the constant (as it wrongly seemed) association with homeless and shiftless boys, as Carson persisted in calling them, had its effect. The defense had done its work well, and Carson had instance after instance to adduce. There were Wood, Allen, and Clibborn to begin with, whose association with Wilde had not been limited to blackmailing him. Wilde liked to talk of the pleasure of feasting with panthers, but these panthers had all been defanged by Queensberry's men, and were ready to say anything to stay free. If they often mixed up what they had done with Wilde with what they had done with Douglas, so much the better.

As Carson began to sink his teeth into Wilde, Clarke realized he must do something. Up to now he had withheld Queensberry's letters to his son and ex-wife, but he now read them out as evidence. They proved that Queensberry was beside himself, but they also reasserted the wholesome fatherliness of his motives. On 1 April 1894 Queensberry had admonished his son for doing nothing, and for being intimate with Wilde. In the second letter, in answer to Douglas's telegram 'What a funny little man you are', Queensberry threatened to thrash Douglas, and to create a public scandal if he caught him again with Wilde. On 6 July he wrote his father-in-law, Alfred Montgomery, complaining of his ex-wife's support of Alfred Douglas. 'Your daughter must be mad by the way she is behaving . . . I am now fully convinced that the Rosebery-Gladstone-Royal insult that came to me through my other son, that she worked that . . .' On 21 August 1894, in reply to a vicious postcard from his son, he said in part, 'You reptile. You are no son of mine and I never thought you were.' And on 28 August he wrote to 'You miserable creature . . . If you are my son, it is only confirming proof to me, if I needed any, how right I was to face every horror and misery I have done rather than run the risk of bringing more creatures into the world like yourself, and that was the entire and only reason of my breaking with your mother as a wife, so intensely was I dissatisfied with her as the mother of you children, and particularly yourself, whom, when quite a baby I cried over you the bitterest tears a man ever shed, that I had brought such a creature into the world, and unwittingly committed such a crime. If you are not my son, and in the Christian country with these hypocrites 'tis a wise father who knows his own child, and no wonder on the principles they intermarry on . . . You must be demented; there is madness on your mother's side.'

The effect of these letters was not what Clarke intended. According to Marjoribanks, who must have got it from Carson, the introduction of the names of

Rosebery and Gladstone, which at once appeared in the continental press, made it inevitable that Wilde should be tried when the Queensberry case was over, in case it looked as if these men had favored him out of a need to protect themselves.

In any case the letters did not stop the merciless march of Carson through Wilde's liaisons. There were Charley Parker and his brother, one a valet, the other a groom, whom Wilde had met through Taylor. Asked if he knew their occupations, Wilde replied, 'I did not know it, but if I had I should not have cared. I didn't care twopence what they were. I liked them. I have a passion to civilise the community.' This was the opposite of his condemnation of the general reading public, and Carson was quick to fasten upon 'the valet and the groom' as strange companions for an artist. Then there was Fred Atkins, whom Wilde had taken with him to Paris. There was Ernest Scarfe, whom he had met through Taylor. There was Sidney Mavor, who stayed at the Albemarle Hotel with Wilde one night. Carson came at last to Walter Grainger, a servant at a house in the High Street, Oxford, where Douglas had rooms. 'Did you ever kiss him?' 'Oh, dear no. He was a peculiarly plain boy. He was, unfortunately, extremely ugly. I pitied him for it.'

CARSON: Was that the reason why you did not kiss him?

WILDE: Oh, Mr Carson, you are pertinently insolent.

CARSON: Why, sir, did you mention that this boy was extremely ugly?

WILDE: For this reason. If I were asked why I did not kiss a door-mat, I should say because I do not like to kiss door-mats. I do not know why I mentioned that he was ugly, except that I was stung by the insolent question you put to me and the way you have insulted me through this hearing. Am I to be cross-examined because I do not like it?

Carson persisted, and at last Wilde answered, 'You sting me and insult me and try to unnerve me; and at times one says things flippantly when one ought to speak more seriously. I admit it.' Carson went on to the Savoy, and asked whether an incident involving buggery had occurred. Wilde denied it absolutely. Carson returned to Atkins and Charley Parker, and took up various presents made to them and other boys. He then turned to Edward Shelley. Wilde denied any wrongdoing, and in rebuttal Clarke read letters written by Shelley asking Wilde for help and expressing admiration for his writings. Carson then ended with some questions about Conway and Wood. The exchange of letters between Humphreys and

Queensberry in 1894 was read, and Carson also made clear that the 'exalted personages' – that is, Rosebery, Gladstone, and the Queen, were not mentioned in relation to the question of Wilde's sodomy. It was then time for Carson's opening speech. He said that Queensberry had been animated from the beginning to end 'by one hope alone – that of saving his son.' Wilde, on the other hand, was consorting with 'some of the most immoral characters in London,' such as Taylor, 'a most notorious character – as the police will tell the court.' He vividly contrasted Wilde's artistic élitism with his democratic taste for common boys. On the literary works of Wilde alone, Queensberry's charge would have been justified. But there was also his payment of blackmail to Wood, who was no longer out of the country, but was here and would testify. Carson did not allege any misconduct between Wilde and Douglas. 'God forbid! But everything shows that the young man was in a dangerous position in that he acquiesced in the domination of Mr Wilde, a man of great ability and attainments.' (Queensberry had succeeded in protecting his son.) He was now going to bring forward the young men, who would testify to 'shocking acts' with Wilde. Conway, for example, would testify to Wilde's having dressed him up in good clothes, so as to make him appear a fit companion.

At this point Sir Edward Clarke plucked Carson by the gown and with the judge's permission went aside to confer with him. There had been a discussion that morning with Wilde, who was not in court. His solicitor Matthews said that he and Clarke would keep the trial going if Wilde wished so he would have time to get to France. The defense would be allowed to call its witnesses, as a delaying tactic. Otherwise Clarke would have to abandon the prosecution at once. 'I'll stay,' said Wilde. Clarke hoped that Carson would accept a verdict of not guilty, '"not guilty" having reference to the word "posing"' and to *Dorian Gray* and the epigrams in the *Chameleon*. Nothing would then be conceded about Wilde's acts of sodomy as itemized in the Plea of Justification. Wilde agreed, but in the event Carson insisted, and Clarke had to consent, that the whole plea must be allowed, that is, Queensberry was justified in calling Wilde a sodomite in the public interest. The judge instructed the jury so to rule. Queensberry was applauded, and Mr Justice Collins, as Frank Harris noted, made no attempt to stop the cheering, but simply folded up his papers and left. He sent a message to Carson,

Dear Carson

I never heard a more powerful speech nor a more searching crossXam. I congratulate you on having escaped the rest of the filth.

Yrs ever

R. Henn Collins

What made Carson unmade Wilde.

GUIDO: Guilty? – Let those
Who know not what a thing temptation is,
Let those who have not walked as we have done,
In the red fire of passion, those whose lives
Are dull and colourless, in a word let those,
If any such there be, who have not loved,
Cast stones against you.

ON FORTUNE'S WHEEL

The quarry was about to fall. If Queensberry had not brought Wilde down, someone else might well have done so. The easy and half acknowledged indulgence which he practiced with Alfred Douglas's ardent complicity involved a succession of young men, many of them Douglas's castoffs, any one of whom might have toppled Wilde. It was, as Henri de Régnier said, 'a chronological error.' If he had lived in the days of the Greeks, no one would have minded. That summer of 1893, when Douglas, having gone down from Oxford without a degree, joined Wilde at Goring, may stand for many instances of their common imprudence.

In *De Profundis* Wilde brings up the subject of Goring, so as to upbraid Douglas for making him spend the staggering sum of £1,340 in less than a summer. But he says nothing of their riskier joint enterprise, the Philip Danney case. Of it Oscar Browning commented, disingenuously, 'This was the first time I ever heard Oscar was given to those proceedings.'

Wilde had to pick his way among blackmailing boys and furious fathers. He ran a risk with the father of Edward Shelley, John Lane's office employee, who was as indignant as Queensberry, and with the father of a public school boy, Sidney Mavor, just as earlier he had roused the indignation of Frank Miles's father. He was circling nearer to some kind of legal confrontation. Only self-assurance, and the thoughtless flurry of his activities, made him trust to his luck.

Still, the furious fathers mostly stayed in the background, while the blackmailing boys were always about, ready to sell themselves or Wilde. The £35 (probably not £15) he had given to Wood in 1893, in the hope that the young man would go to America and stay there, was not likely to be enough. From America Wood had ominously written, 'Tell Oscar he can send me a draft for an Easter egg.' The gang – for Wood, Allen, Clibborn and others constituted a gang – had obviously marked Wilde for prolonged milking. It was as tricky a game for them as for him, since there were heavier penalties for blackmail than for indecency. Their running such risks fascinated Wilde. Clibborn and Allen, in particular, he admired for waging 'an infamous war against life.' Clibborn liked to tell Wilde of his adventures, and one, with Lord Euston – prominent in the Cleveland Street scandal – required such avaricious tenacity on Clibborn's part as to entitle him, Wilde said, to the Victoria Cross.

Clibborn continued to confide in Wilde as the trial drew near. One day he was telling him, as George Ives recounts, 'the plots that were being planned by threats and money and all kind of means, to bring about his [Wilde's] ruin.' Wilde paid little heed, but suddenly looked up and asked a question that had evidently been long in his mind: 'Bob, what I want to know is, did you ever *love* any boy for his own sake?' Clibborn replied, 'No, Oscar, I can't say I ever did!' For Ives this was an instance of Wilde's mystical search for the truth of things even on the verge of his own collapse. His curiosity was less mystical when he suggested bringing together 'the panther,' as he often called Clibborn, with Ives, who prided himself on being a 'cold disciplined Hellenist,' to see what would happen. But that meeting never took place.

It must be said for Wilde that the risk was impossible to estimate. Society put up with a great deal that was illegal, and sometimes did so knowingly. Countenancing illegality did not amount to sanctioning it, however, and the atmosphere could change at any time. Wilde was dimly aware from the beginning that his genius gave him only a limited immunity. But the way of life which Alfred Douglas had opened up was necessarily reckless. There was something fascinating in being the rival, the accomplice, and the object of each other's love. Shared indiscretion cemented them romantically together. Prudence would have been a form of betrayal.

Events had taken him beyond erotic fantasy and indulgence. After Queensberry's exoneration Wilde was indecisive when others were decisive. Clarke's concession that Wilde's being called a sodomite was in the public interest made prosecution almost certain.
 To be quite sure, Charles Russell, within minutes

of Queensberry's acquittal, addressed a letter to Hamilton Cuffe, Director of Prosecutions,

Dear Sir,

In order that there may be no miscarriage of justice I think it my duty at once to send you a copy of all our witnesses' statements together with a copy of the shorthand notes of the trial.

Queensberry, for his part, informed Wilde, 'I will not prevent your flight, but if you take my son with you, I will shoot you like a dog.' He added, to the French press, 'But I don't think he'll be allowed to go. This case has cost me 30,000 francs, but I don't regret anything, since I know all I have done is for the good of my sons, the honour of my family, and the public benefit.' He said later he had been misquoted; he had said that he would shoot Wilde like a dog, if he had a mind to do so and if it seemed worthwhile. It was probably Queensberry's detectives, rather than Scotland Yard's, who were instructed to stay on Wilde's trail.

That trail led Wilde first to his solicitor Humphreys, then to Sir George Lewis, who threw up his hands and said, 'What is the good of coming to me now?' Then to the Holborn Viaduct Hotel. Douglas, his brother Percy, and Robert Ross accompanied Wilde, and in the hotel he wrote a letter to the editor of the *Evening News*:

It would have been impossible for me to have proved my case without putting Lord Alfred Douglas in the witness-box against his father. Lord Alfred Douglas was extremely anxious to go into the box, but I would not let him do so. Rather than put him in so painful a position I determined to retire from the case, and to bear on my own shoulders whatever ignominy and shame might result from my prosecuting Lord Queensberry.

Oscar Wilde

The letter reads as if Wilde thought the matter might end there. After lunch he gave Ross a cheque to cash for £200 and went on to the Cadogan Hotel, where he was joined by Reggie Turner. Douglas had been staying there for five weeks. Ross and Turner urged Wilde to take a train for Dover and a boat for France, but he seemed incapable of decision. He said 'The train is gone. It is too late.' In fact he still had a chance, but seemed disinclined to take it. Douglas was off trying to see his cousin, the M.P. George Wyndham, and stir up influential friends. Wilde asked Ross to see Constance Wilde and inform her what had happened. She wept and said, 'I hope Oscar is going away abroad.' George Wyndham arrived at four o'clock and asked to see Wilde, but Wilde, fearing recriminations, had Ross talk with him. Wyndham began to scold Ross for allowing Wilde and Douglas to be together, but Ross disarmed him by saying that he and all Wilde's friends had been trying to separate them for years. Wyndham changed his tack and asked Ross to persuade Wilde to leave the country at once. They were still talking when Douglas rushed in, and took Wyndham off to see someone who might help.

At five o'clock a sympathetic reporter from the *Star* arrived and told Ross that the warrant for Wilde's arrest had been issued. In fact, Charles Russell had busily gone round to see Sir John Bridge at Bow Street in the early afternoon and persuaded him that Wilde should be arrested. Ross told Wilde, who 'went very grey in the face.' Up to now he had not let Ross give him the money from the bank, but he now asked for it, and Ross thought he must have decided upon flight. Instead Wilde settled down in his chair and said, 'I shall stay and do my sentence whatever it is.'

A half-packed suitcase lay on the bed, emblem of contradictory impulses. He was tired of action. Like Hamlet, as he understood that hero, he wished to distance himself from his plight, to be the spectator of

his own tragedy. His stubbornness, his courage, and his gallantry also kept him there. He had always met adversity head on, to face hostile journalists, moralistic reviewers, and canting, ranting fathers. A man so concerned with his image disdained to think of himself as a fugitive, skulking in dark corners instead of lording it in the limelight. He preferred to be a great figure, doomed by fate and the unjust laws of a foreign country. Suffering was more becoming than embarrassment. Writers, after all, had been prisoners before him. Cunninghame Graham and Blunt came to mind. His mind would survive, superior to any indignities his inferiors could heap upon him. If he was to be immolated, so must be his age. Reveal him as pederast, reveal his society as hypocrite. So he waited, defiant. At ten past six came the expected knock at the door. A waiter entered, followed by two detectives. They said, 'We have a warrant here, Mr Wilde, for your arrest on a charge of committing indecent acts.' Wilde asked if he would be given bail and the detectives were doubtful. As he rose and groped unsteadily for his overcoat and for a book with a yellow cover, it was suddenly evident that he had been drinking heavily. He asked Ross to get him a change of clothes and bring
 it to him. 'Where shall I be taken?' he asked. 'To Bow

Street,' was the reply. The cab drove off, and the Wilde epoch came to an end.

DESPAIR AND ITS ANODYNES

Every great love has its tragedy, and now ours has too.

Ross went as directed to Tite Street. Mrs Wilde had locked the bedroom door and library and gone out. Wilde's servant, Arthur, was there, and helped Ross to break into the bedroom and pack a bag. At Bow Street he was refused admission, either to see Wilde or to leave the clothing. He realized that Wilde's papers were in danger from Queensberry's men or the police, and hurried back to Tite Street. Again with Arthur's help, he broke open the library door, and removed some of Wilde's letters and manuscripts. He noted grimly that the two most recent writings, *A Florentine Tragedy* and an enlarged version of 'The Portrait of Mr W.H.,' which had been returned to Wilde a few days before, were not to be found. (Both survived.) After all this, Ross drove to his mother's house and collapsed.

Ross was named in the newspapers as having been

with Wilde at the time of the arrest and had to resign from some of his clubs. Mrs Ross was understandably alarmed for her son and insisted that he go abroad. He demurred on the grounds that he would be abandoning his friend, and she offered £500 to help in Wilde's defense if he would leave at once. He allowed himself to be persuaded, and took himself off to the Terminus Hotel at Calais and a week later to Rouen. Reggie Turner and Maurice Schwabe also decamped. Henry Harland wrote to Edmund Gosse that six hundred gentlemen had crossed from Dover to Calais on a night when normally only sixty would have done so. Douglas, however, elected to stay on, though he appeared to be in greater danger than the others. In fact, his father had evidently resolved to protect him, probably by having Russell arrange matters with the Director of Prosecutions. Robert Sherard and Ada and Ernest Leverson were the other friends of Wilde who remained conspicuously loyal and helpful. But dozens fell away.

Wilde left a message for Douglas that he would be at Bow Street Police Station that night, and asked him to try to get his brother Percy, and George Alexander and Lewis Waller (from the theatres where Wilde's plays were running), to attend next morning to give bail. Only Percy was willing. Wilde also asked Douglas to secure Humphreys' services for the hearings. Douglas went round to Bow Street in the evening in the hope of seeing Wilde, but like Ross he was refused. He resolved, however, to see him every day. For his part, Wilde ate a bit of cold chicken, drank some coffee, was refused permission to smoke, and spent a wretched night.

'With what a crash this fell!' Wilde wrote to the Leversons on 9 April. It was like the history of Timon of Athens, or of Wilde's old admiration, *Agamemnon*, yet meaner. Wilde's name was removed from the hoardings of the two theatres where *An Ideal Husband* and *The Importance of Being Earnest* were playing to large audiences, and soon, with public feeling running high, the plays were taken off. The same thing happened in New York, and the actress Rose Coghlan, who was about to take *A Woman of No Importance* on tour in the United States, cancelled it. Not only did Wilde's friends in England drop away; so did most of his friends in France. On 13 April 1895 Jules Huret, in his '*Petite chronique des lettres*' in *Le Figaro littéraire*, named three French writers as Wilde's intimates: Catulle Mendès, Marcel Schwob, and Jean Lorrain. A furore resulted. Schwob sent his seconds to meet

Huret's seconds, and was angry when they accepted Huret's explanation. Lorrain had Huret publish a letter from him denying intimacy, and forgot having dedicated his story, 'Lanterne magique', to Wilde in *L'Echo de Paris* of 14 December 1891. Catulle Mendès was not so easily fobbed off. He and Huret had a duel with épées in the 'premières feuilles' of the forest of St Germain, on 17 April at 3 p.m. Blood was shed, but as a commentator remarked, in droplets only. Colette's husband, Willy, registered his amusement in *L'Echo de Paris* for 17 April at Wilde's behavior and England's embarrassment over it; but on 20 April Henry Bauer mocked Willy for pretending that homosexuality was only an English vice. 'I will not disavow now having known and visited him,' he said. Wilde's heteroclite tastes were not his affair. Nor had Wilde done any harm: 'Young Douglas was old enough to go out without his governess, and without his father's permission.' Octave Mirbeau also wrote sympathetically of Wilde in an article, '*A Propos du* "Hard Labour."' As for Sarah Bernhardt, when Sherard asked her to buy the rights to *Salome* for $1,500 to $2,000 to cover court costs, she expressed sympathy, dithered, and did nothing.

If Wilde hoped that the hearings that began on 6

April would soon be over, he was mistaken. They dragged on and on, with intervals of several days between each. Meanwhile he was in Bow Street in physical pain, never saying a word to the other prisoners, making subdued groans as he changed his standing position from time to time. He was then transferred to Holloway Prison except when recalled for another hearing. He hoped for bail, and the magistrate had it in his power to grant it. But Sir John Bridge was revolted by the crime of sodomy. As the French newspapers commented with some bewilderment, in England sodomy ranked only one step below murder. Though Humphreys pointed out that Wilde could have run away if he had wanted to, Bridge insisted that the gravity of the charge made bail unthinkable.

Wilde's second hearing took place on 11 April, the third on 18 April. The Grand Jury found true bills against Wilde and Alfred Taylor, whose case was linked with Wilde's very much against Wilde's interest, on 23 April. The charges were indecency and sodomy. Meanwhile various incidents added to the tensions. On 11 April a stationer tried to sell photographs of Wilde; the resulting fracas made the police intervene and stop the sale. On 24 April, a bankruptcy sale of Wilde's effects was forced by Queensberry, who demanded payment of his £600 costs, and by other creditors who followed his lead. Douglas had promised that his family would pay the costs of the trial; they did not. Wilde was rendered miserable by the sale not only of his manuscripts and his own books, but of presentation volumes from Hugo, Whitman, Swinburne, Mallarmé, Morris, and Verlaine, his Burne-Jones and Whistler drawings, paintings by Monticelli and Simeon Solomon, expensive china, Thomas Carlyle's writing desk and a hundred other things. A few were bought by friends. There was still not enough money to pay off the debts, so the estate remained in receivership until Ross eventually rescued it, long after Wilde's death.

At the dismal proceedings Wilde was represented by young Travers Humphreys and later by Sir Edward Clarke, who offered to represent him without fee. The prosecutor was Charles Gill, like Carson a Trinity College, Dublin man, and equally prejudiced against Wilde. There was some effort by the prosecution to persuade Taylor to turn state's evidence and so get off, but, perhaps because Wilde had talked to him before the trial, Taylor refused to betray his friend in any way. A long array of witnesses was produced, headed by the infamous Parker brothers, who claimed they had been recruited by Taylor to minister to Wilde's wishes. At first Charles Parker pretended to be nineteen; under cross-examination he proved to be twenty-one. In fact, none of the young men was under the statutory age of seventeen. There was testimony from Taylor's fellow-tenants and landladies about his peculiarly curtained and perfumed rooms, and the young men who came to tea there. Alfred Wood the blackmailer was there to testify about receiving £35 from Wilde in exchange for the letters Wilde had sent to Douglas, who had failed to remove them from his clothes before giving them to Wood. Sidney (better known as Jenny) Mavor had been threatened into testifying, but Douglas managed to collar him before his appearance and to remind him that he was a public school boy with a sense of honor, counselling him to deny having anything to do with Wilde. So this young man, asked what had happened the time he spent a night in Wilde's bed, replied, 'Nothing.'

The Savoy Hotel was represented by its 'professor of massage', Antonio Migge, who testified to having seen a young man sleeping in Wilde's bed while Wilde was dressing. The chambermaid Jane Cotter also claimed to have seen a boy there. A former housekeeper at the hotel, Mrs Perkins, testified that there had been fecal stains on the bedsheets. As for Taylor, there was testimony that he had gone through a form of marriage, dressed as a woman. The more Sir John Bridge heard of this testimony, the more he bristled, and when asked again for bail he said that 'no worse crime than this' existed, and bail could not be allowed. After the Grand Jury presented its charge, Wilde's lawyers asked that the case be postponed until the May Sessions, to give the defense time to prepare and to allow public opinion to die down. The prosecutor, Gill, objected, and Mr Justice Charles, who was to hear the case, agreed to an immediate trial, beginning on 26 April, promising it would be a fair one.

Douglas on 19 April sent a letter to the *Star*, complaining that Wilde was being judged before his trial, not at it. What was only too clear about this and subsequent letters from him to the press was that he was thinking more about himself than about his friend, and Wilde in *De Profundis* was severe on the subject: 'they [the letters] were simply to say that you hated your father. Nobody cared if you did or not.'

No doubt such thoughts glanced off his mind at the time. Mostly he was conscious only of Douglas's love for him, and his for Douglas. The almost daily visits meant a great deal. They were limited to about fifteen minutes, and there was so much noise that Wilde, who was rather deaf in one ear, could hardly hear. Wilde informed the Leversons on 9 April, 'I write to you from prison, where your kind words have reached me and given me comfort, though they have made me cry, in my loneliness. Not that I am really alone. A slim thing, goldhaired like an angel, stands always at my side. His presence overshadows me. He moves in the gloom like a white flower . . . I thought but to defend him from his father: I thought of nothing else, and now –.' To Ross and his close friend More Adey (translator of Ibsen's *Brand* and an art expert), both at Calais, he wrote on 9 April, 'Bosie is so wonderful. I think of nothing else. I saw him yesterday.' To Ada Leverson he wrote on 17 April, 'As for me, the wings of great love encompass me: holy ground.' As his trial approached, he wrote to her, 'I care less when I think that he is thinking of me. I think of nothing else.' In the meantime he sent Douglas a number of passionate letters.

But Sir Edward Clarke felt that Douglas's presence at the trial would be prejudicial to Wilde's interests, as stirring up recollections of the supposed corruption of the young man by him. Douglas would not go without Wilde's express request, and insisted upon having it in writing. At the last meeting, Douglas recalled, Wilde 'kissed the end of my finger through an iron grating at Newgate, and he begged me to let nothing in the world alter my attitude and my conduct towards him.' The young man joined Ross and Turner at the Hôtel Terminus in Calais, then went on to Rouen and Paris. He told the press that he had gone because of his mother's illness in Italy, but this pretext was quickly exploded. To a reporter for *Le Journal*, on 25 May 1895, he said that there had been danger of his being called as a witness, presumably by the prosecution, which he did not want. But in his *Autobiography*, Douglas said that on the third day of the trial he telegraphed certain information to Sir Edward Clarke, though it was prejudicial to himself, and again offered to give evidence. Presumably he took responsibility for the incidents of buggery, since Wilde did not practice this. The solicitors replied that his telegram was very improper, and that he should not make Clarke's task more difficult than it was already. Wilde wrote to him on the last day of the trial, 29 April:

My dearest boy, This is to assure you of my immortal, my eternal love for you. Tomorrow all will be over. If prison and dishonour be my destiny, think that my love for you and this idea, this still more divine belief, that you love me in return will sustain me in my unhappiness and will make me capable, I hope, of bearing my grief most patiently. Since the hope, nay rather the certainty, of meeting you again in some world is the goal and the encouragement of my present life, ah! I must continue to live in this world because of that . . . If one day, at Corfu or in some enchanted isle, there were a little house where we could live together, oh! life would be sweeter than it has ever been. Your love has broad wings and is strong, your love comes to me through my prison bars and comforts me, your love is the light of all my hours. Those who know not what love is will write, I know, if fate is against us, that I have had a bad influence upon your life. If they do that, you shall write, you shall say in your turn, that it is not so. Our love was always beautiful and noble, and if I have been the butt of a terrible tragedy, it is because the nature of that love has not been understood. In your letter this morning you say something which gives me courage. I must remember it. You write that it is my duty to you and to myself to live in spite of everything. I think that is true. I shall try and I shall do it . . . I stretch out my hands towards you, Oh! may I live to touch your hair and your hands.

WILDE'S FIRST TRIAL

The form of government that is most suitable to the artist is no government at all.

The trial, which opened on 26 April 1895, went over the same ground as the Queensberry trial and the three hearings at Bow Street, and perhaps never in the Nineties was so much unsavory evidence given so much publicity. The prosecutor insisted upon a speedy trial, in which the cases of Taylor and Wilde would be joined because Taylor had procured young men to commit acts of indecency with Wilde. So some charges related to conspiracy. Mr Justice Sir Arthur Charles agreed, over Clarke's protest, but eventually the conspiracy charges were dropped voluntarily by the prosecution, and the judge then said he had never felt that they were properly joined to the other charges. Taylor, a bad witness (as Beerbohm says), and badly represented by J. T. Grein, was simply an additional weight on Wilde's head. In other respects the case was conducted by the Treasury with considerable hypocrisy. Not only was homosexuality common in the English public schools which most of the legal personages present had attended. Also there had evidently been an agreement between Gill and Charles Russell, Queensberry's solicitor, that Douglas's name would be kept out of the case as far as possible in return for Queensberry's detailed evidence against Wilde. Who it was who introduced Atkins and Mavor to Wilde remained a mystery, though clearly a soluble one. As to why none of the important people whom George Wyndham approached saw fit to prevent the trial, there was a reluctance to interfere with the course of justice, and a lack of appetite to take on Queensberry as an adversary. There was also the old difficulty that Rosebery's name had been mentioned in one of Queensberry's letters. George Ives heard, nonetheless, that Rosebery had considered doing something to help Wilde until Balfour told him, 'If you do, you will lose the election.' (In the event, he lost the election anyway.) Everyone seemed to have a reason for leaning over backwards to avoid any suggestion of going easy on Wilde. As for Lockwood, the Solicitor-General, Carson is said to have suggested that he leave Wilde alone, as having suffered enough, but Lockwood said he had no alternative but to continue what Carson had initiated.

Wilde looked thin; his hair had been cut shorter than

usual. He was, said the *New York Times*, 'careworn and anxious.' His cross-examination had few surprises to offer. He admitted that he knew the boys who had testified, but not that he had had indecent relations with them. The serious addition to the charges had to do with one young man who was not a prostitute, Edward Shelley. His testimony, given with extreme discomfort, was somewhat vitiated by his admission that he had at times been out of his mind, and also by the fact that he had pursued Wilde's friendship and asked his help long after he had supposedly been corrupted by him.

In cross-examining Wilde, Gill tried to follow Carson's lead and besmirch him by association with the *Chameleon*, not so much with 'The Priest and the Acolyte' as with two homosexual poems by Douglas in it. 'What is the "Love that dare not speak its name"?' he asked. After all his lies, denials, and shifts, Wilde suddenly found a voice:

The 'Love that dare not speak its name' in this century is such a great affection of an elder for a younger man as there was between David and Jonathan, such as Plato made the very basis of his philosophy, and such as you find in the sonnets of Michaelangelo and Shakespeare. It is that deep, spiritual affection that is as pure as it is perfect. It dictates and pervades great works of art like those of Shakespeare and Michaelangelo, and those two letters of mine, such as they are. It is in this century misunderstood, so much misunderstood that it may be described as the 'Love that dare not speak its name,' and on account of it I am placed where I am now. It is beautiful, it is fine, it is the noblest form of affection. There is nothing unnatural about it. It is intellectual, and it repeatedly exists between an elder and a younger man, when the elder man has intellect, and the younger man has all the joy, hope and glamour of life before him. That it should be so the world does not understand. The world mocks at it and sometimes puts one in the pillory for it.

This *cri de coeur* had its effect, though it could not, as the prosecutor noted, apply to the male prostitutes in the case, and Wilde himself said it could only happen once in a lifetime. For once Wilde spoke not wittily but well. As Max Beerbohm wrote to Reggie Turner after attending the trial, 'Oscar has been quite superb. His speech about the Love that dares not tell his name was simply wonderful and carried the whole court right away, quite a tremendous burst of applause. Here was this man, who had been for a month in prison and loaded with insults and crushed and buffeted, perfectly self-possessed, dominating the Old Bailey with his fine presence and musical voice. He has never had so great a triumph, I am sure, as when the gallery burst into applause – I am sure it affected the jury.'

The rest of the cross-examination went less favorably. Wilde had again to defend his letters to Douglas. As for the evidence of the hotel servants, Wilde said, 'It is entirely untrue. Can I answer for what hotel servants say years after I have left the hotel?' He denied all Shelley's evidence of impropriety, as well as the Parkers', Atkins's, and Wood's.

Why did you take up with these youths? – I am a lover of youth. (Laughter)

You exalt youth as a sort of god? – I like to study the young in everything. There is something fascinating in youthfulness.

So you would prefer puppies to dogs and kittens to cats? – I think so. I should enjoy, for instance, the society of a beardless, briefless barrister quite as much as that of the most accomplished Q.C. (Laughter)

This time Sir Edward Clarke was better prepared. He persuasively denied that *Dorian Gray* or 'Phrases and Philosophies for the Use of the Young' was in any sense corrupting or corrupted. He pointed out that Wilde, instead of shrinking like a guilty man from public exposure, had sought publicity by prosecuting

Lord Queensberry. As to the hotel evidence against Wilde, it was extraordinary that the prosecution had been able to find such a paucity of it, when Wilde had stayed in hotel after hotel for years. The evidence of the Parkers, of Wood, and of Atkins obviously superimposed on what was true much that was false, as the best lies do. Wilde was undoubtedly taken in by them, which was evidence of imprudence not crime. They were blackmailers whose evidence could not be trusted. Atkins had been proved on the stand to have perjured himself. 'I ask the jury,' Clarke said, 'to clear from this frightful imputation one of our most renowned and accomplished men of letters of today, and in clearing him, to clear society from a stain.' Grein then made a weak defense of Taylor. Gill, for the prosecution, insisted that the letters to Douglas 'breathe an unholy passion,' and that Wilde's admitted presents to these many boys were proof of his gratitude. As Ives commented in his journal, Wilde suffered because of his generosity, which was not confined to young men. Granted that some of the boys were not of the highest type, there was still the case of Shelley, whose testimony was not tainted by blackmail charges. Finally, Gill gave up the charges of conspiracy. The case now went to the judge.

Mr Justice Charles agreed to omit the conspiracy charges, and to direct a verdict of acquittal upon them. On the literary question he proved enlightened. He was inclined to agree with Clarke that Wilde was not culpable for having written *Dorian Gray* or for the *Chameleon* pieces which he had not written. As to the letters to Douglas, he was not inclined to accept Gill's statement that these proved anything. He acknowledged that Shelley was unstable. He found the stories of the maids and other functionaries at the Savoy Hotel difficult to credit. As to the fecal stains, he pointed out that these might have an innocent explanation. The judge did not however reject the testimony of the witnesses about Wilde's and Taylor's behavior. He put four questions to the jury:

1) Do you think that Wilde committed indecent acts with Edward Shelley and Alfred Wood and with a person or persons unknown at the Savoy Hotel or with Charles Parker?
2) Did Taylor procure or attempt to procure the commission of these acts or of any of them?
3) Did Wilde and Taylor or either of them attempt to get Atkins to commit indecencies?
4) Did Taylor commit indecent acts with Charles Parker or with William Parker?

The jury was out from 1.35 to 5.15 p.m. They then reported that they could agree only on the question about Atkins, where their verdict was not guilty. One newspaper, *L'Echo de Paris* of 4 May, said that the vote to convict Wilde had been ten to two, as revealed by an indiscreet juror in a Pall Mall club, while Max Beerbohm heard that it was eleven to one, and Alfred Douglas agreed that only one juror voted for acquittal. Beerbohm reported to More Adey, 'Hoscar stood very upright when he was brought up to hear the verdict and looked most leonine and sphinx-like. I pitied poor little Alfred Taylor – nobody remembered his existence . . . Hoscar is thinner and in consequence finer to look at. Willie [Wilde] has been extracting fivers from Humphreys. It was horrible leaving the court day after day and having to pass through a knot of renters (the younger Parker wearing Her Majesty's uniform, another form of female attire) who were allowed to hang around after giving their evidence and to wink at likely persons.'

Owing to the jury's failure to reach a verdict, a new trial was ordered. The judge again refused bail, but Clarke announced he would seek it from another judge in chambers. Clarke proposed that the next trial be postponed, but Gill said it would be the usual course to hold it in the next sessions, and the judge agreed. Many people urged that harm 'would be done to the public morals' if the case were renewed. T. M. Healy begged Lockwood not to put Wilde on trial again. Lockwood said, 'I would not but for the abominable rumours against Rosebery.' So the long drawn-out farce went into its third and last act.

BETWEEN TRIALS

What are called criminals nowadays are not
criminals at all.

Bereft of the company of his lover Douglas, and his friends Ross and Turner – all three fugitive in the Hôtel de la Poste in Rouen – and unsought by most of his other friends, Wilde could feel the shades of the prison house drawing round him figuratively as well as literally. He had twenty-five days to go before his second trial ended. The first five were spent in Holloway Prison. There was now no reason to deny him bail, but Mr Justice Charles perhaps wished to indicate that he had no sympathy for pederasts, even
 those who might be innocent. Yet only a misdemeanor,

not a felony, was involved, so bail could not long be refused. Two days later, on 3 May, Charles Matthews applied again on Wilde's behalf, this time to Mr Baron Pollock in chambers, for bail until the new trial should begin. He proposed two sureties of £1,000 each.

On 4 May Pollock set bail at £5,000, of which £2,500 would be allowed to Wilde on his own recognizance. It took two days to round up sureties for the remaining £2,500. Frank Harris says he volunteered, but was ruled ineligible because he was not a householder. Bosie's brother Percy had no money in hand, but out of loyalty to Bosie scraped together half of what was required in defiance of his father. The other half was harder. It may have been Ernest Leverson who, being himself debarred by the terms of his business partnership from going bail for anyone, approached first Selwyn Image, who did not have the money, and then the Reverend Stewart Headlam, who did. Headlam – whom Wilde had privately dubbed 'the heresiarch' – was scarcely acquainted with him, having met him only twice, but he was a man of conviction, and strongly supported the view that Wilde was entitled not to be prejudged. Being a socialist and an unorthodox Christian, he knew that he would suffer notoriety for his kind of action, and worse, be thought to have sought it. His maid left his service, some of his friends defected, and an enemy accused him of wading in Gomorrah on his way to building Jerusalem. At least there would be no financial loss if Wilde jumped bail; so Leverson had promised, and Wilde gave his word not to flee. With Headlam's £1,225 and Percy Douglas's in hand, all impediments to bail were removed. The bail hearing at Bow Street Police Station on 7 May concluded with Wilde's release.

Where to go was not so easily decided. Two rooms had been engaged for him at the Midland Hotel at St Pancras, far from his usual haunts, but just as he was sitting down to a late dinner, the manager entered. 'You are Oscar Wilde, I believe.' Wilde did not disavow it. 'You must leave the hotel at once.' Some of Queensberry's pugilistic roughnecks, egged on by the Marquess himself, had threatened the manager with reprisals for receiving Wilde, and they followed him as he drove across town to another hotel. There too, after a few minutes, the manager apologized, but said that some men had threatened to sack the hotel and raise the street against Wilde if he did not leave at once. By now it was near midnight. In the end Wilde had no alternative but to go to the house where his

 brother Willie was living with his second wife, Lily

Lees, and Lady Wilde, 146 Oakley Street. It was not pleasant to have to plead with his brother, to whom he had not spoken for a year and a half, 'Willie, give me shelter or I shall die in the streets.' As Willie described the scene later, 'He came tapping with his beak against the window-pane, and fell down on my threshold like a wounded stag.' For the moment magnanimity was in order.

Willie gave his brother a room with a small camp-bed in a corner between the fireplace and the wall, and here for some days Oscar was physically ill. His friends in France heard about it and asked Robert Sherard to go over and see him. Sherard did so. He found Wilde's face 'flushed and swollen.' 'Oh, why have you brought me no poison from Paris?' he asked alliteratively in a broken voice. Sherard offered to take him to the country to recover his health, but he did not want to move. Sherard managed to rouse him by proposing they read some Wordsworth; in one sonnet Wordsworth was caught out rhyming 'love' with 'shove,' and Wilde feigned outrage and said severely to the hapless descendant, 'Robert, what does this mean?'

It soon became apparent that the family setting in Oakley Street would prove anything but easy. Willie was setting up as a moralist: 'At least my vices were decent,' he muttered in his cups. He told Oscar that he was defending him all over London, at which Oscar commented to a friend, 'My poor, dear brother, he would compromise a steam engine.' 'Willie makes such a merit of giving me shelter,' he told Harris, and confided that, as Beerbohm had said, his brother had sold old letters to Humphreys in what amounted to blackmail. For his part, Willie had his own rhythmical explanations of his brother's fall: 'It is his vanity that has brought all this disgrace upon him; they swung incense before him, they swung it before his heart.' Both Willie and Lady Wilde were determined that Oscar should stay and stand trial; Willie would assure visitors, 'Oscar is an Irish gentleman, and he will face the music.' As for Lady Wilde, she declaimed to Oscar in her grand manner, 'If you stay, even if you go to prison, you will always be my son. It will make no difference to my affection. But if you go, I will never speak to you again.' Wilde promised her that he would stay.

But as he approached martyrdom his friends wished to deny him it. Percy, though one of his guarantors, declared, 'It will practically ruin me if I lose all that money at the present moment, but if there is a chance even of conviction, in God's name let him go.' Sherard urged Wilde to leave, and Frank Harris brought matters to a head. Harris insisted upon taking Wilde out to lunch, against Willie's wishes, and proposed the Café Royal, scene of so many meals in the past. Oscar did not feel it would be seemly, so Harris brought him instead to a restaurant in Great Portland Street, where they had a private room. Harris wanted to stiffen Wilde's resistance. He proposed that Wilde should say he liked the company of young men because he liked writing about them. Wilde did not respond, and never adopted this tactic. Harris described the testimony as a pack of lies, and Wilde said that the testimony of the chambermaids at the Savoy Hotel was based on their mixing up his room with Douglas's. Harris offered to make a plan of the rooms and get the maids to admit their error, but Wilde did not want Douglas to be implicated. At any rate, he said, Shelley's testimony remained, and the judge had said that this was unimpugnable. Harris declared that Shelley was an accomplice, and therefore could not be believed without corroboration, of which there was none. At this Wilde broke out, and said, 'You talk with passion and conviction, as if I were innocent.' 'But you are innocent,' said Harris, 'aren't you?' 'No,' said Wilde. 'I thought you knew that all along.' Harris said, 'I did not believe it for a moment.' 'This will make a great difference to you?' asked Wilde, but Harris assured him it would not.

He now developed his fallback plan, that Wilde should escape. A Jewish businessman of his acquaintance happened to mention owning a yacht, and Harris asked him if he would rent it for a month. The man was willing, and asked what Harris planned to do. On impulse Harris told him exactly what he wanted it for, and the yachtsman then said, 'In that case you can have it for nothing.' He too wanted Wilde to escape. Harris now made his proposal to Wilde. The yacht was at Erith, he said, and they could leave at once. Much scepticism has been shown about this yacht, yet both Yeats and Ada Leverson knew of the plan, and it seems to have been available even if it was not waiting at Erith with steam up, as Harris dramatically pictured it. Wilde, however, refused to go.

It was while he was still in Oakley Street that the Leversons invited Wilde to dinner, and discovered how unhappy he was, living with his brother. They bravely invited him to stay with them, and he accepted. Before he arrived with his belongings, they called the servants together and offered them a month's wages if they wished to leave rather than be in the house with this notorious man. All chose to stay with 'poor Mr Wilde,' as one called him, and Mrs Leverson drove over to Oakley Street to fetch him, on about 18 May. The address was kept secret to ward Queensberry off. The Leversons' son was in the country, so Wilde was shown up to the nursery, which consisted of two large rooms and a bathroom. 'Shall I remove the toys?' she asked, but he replied, 'Please leave them.' So among the rocking horses and doll's houses he received his solicitors and friends, gathering the threads of destitution and disgrace. To avoid embarrassing his hosts he took his meals upstairs and did not come down until six o'clock. Then he appeared in dinner clothes, flower in buttonhole, and made a point of talking to Mrs Leverson about everything but his main concerns. His old hairdresser came to shave him and wave his hair every day.

Later Mrs Leverson would remember some of his conversation. He had romantic ideas about absinthe, and described its effect to her: 'After the first glass, you see things as you wish they were. After the second, you see things as they are not. Finally you see things as they really are, and that is the most horrible thing in the world.' 'How do you mean?' 'I mean disassociated. Take a top-hat! You think you see it as it really is. But you don't, because you associate it with other things and ideas. If you had never heard of one before, and suddenly saw it alone, you'd be frightened, or laugh. That is the effect absinthe has, and that is why it drives men mad.' He went on, 'Three nights I sat up all night drinking absinthe, and thinking that I was singularly clearheaded and sane. The waiter came in and began watering the sawdust. The most wonderful flowers, tulips, lilies, and roses sprang up and made a garden of the café. "Don't you see them?" I said to him. "*Mais, non, monsieur, il n'y a rien.*"' There was no drug to make the world flower now. He turned to other subjects, especially books. Dickens was an old phobia, and it was to amuse her he made his classic remark, 'One must have a heart of stone to read the death of Little Nell without laughing.' Or he made up unChristian parables in the manner of *Lives of the Saints*. He liked one or another of these well enough to ask for something to write it down, but Mrs Leverson could not put her hand on anything. 'You have all the equipment of a writer, my dear Sphinx,' he said to her, 'except pens, ink and paper.'

While Oscar Wilde was with the Leversons, Yeats came on 19 May to Oakley Street in search of him. Yeats's father had told him he owed it to Wilde to offer to testify for him, or do some service, and Yeats brought along a packet of letters he had collected from Irish men of letters, including George Russell, to encourage his friend. (Only Professor Edward Dowden refused.) He was met, however, by Willie, who said, 'Before I give him this, you must tell me what is in it. Are you telling him to run away? All his friends are telling him that, and we have made up our minds that he must go to prison if necessary.' Yeats replied, 'No, I certainly would not advise him to run away.' Which was true: to Yeats it seemed a great moment for Wilde to show his mettle. He wrote to Dowden about his visit:

I went to try and see Wilde today and to tell him how much I sympathised with him in his trouble. He has left Oakley Street but they told me this much about his movements. A yacht and a very large sum of money was placed at his disposal and all settled for his flight but he refused to go. He says he will stand it out and face the worst and no matter how it turns out work on. He will not go down, they said, or drink, or take poison. I mentioned how I had found some of our Dublin literary men sympathetic to him and my words were received with most pathetic gentleness and I promised to tell them about his plans. I write to suggest that you either write direct to him, some sympathetic words,

Morris has already written, or write some answer to this which I can get shown to him.

Others were keener than Yeats and Willie to save him from prison, however it might spoil the drama. Constance Wilde came to see her husband at the Leversons' and spent two hours with him. She brought an earnest message from her lawyer, imploring him to go away before his next trial, which would undoubtedly be calamitous. She left in tears, and Ada Leverson saw on his face 'a look of immovable obstinacy.' Mrs Leverson herself had the temerity to send up a note asking him to do what his wife urged. There was no reply until he came down to dinner, when he handed her back her note, only remarking, 'That is not like you, Sphinx,' before he changed the subject.

Wilde had made a decision, and intended to stick to it. Mrs Leverson thought him too involved in a fantasy of success to believe that anything bad could happen to him, but Wilde's life had offered no such cycle of triumphs as she supposed. There had been his broken engagement to Florence Balcombe, his removal from Frank Miles's house, the failure of his early plays, his troubled American lecture tour, years of not having enough money, and the chaotic affair with Douglas. As he was to declare later, his works had always had a telltale undercurrent of sorrow. And he knew what running away would be like, whether he did it in the boisterous company of Frank Harris or by himself. There would be no dignity in that. He might well be stopped, or if not stopped, he would have to slink about the Continent as a fugitive from British justice. As his trip to Florence had shown, slinking was not Wilde's style. Ostracism (a subject about which he had quarreled with Jebb years before) was not for him. What he wrote to Douglas just before the trial ended was what he felt all along: 'I decided that it was nobler and more beautiful to stay . . . I did not want to be called a coward or a deserter. A false name, a disguise, a hunted life, all that is not for me.' He chose to be convicted, knowing that people would wrongly say that he chose out of weakness or megalomania – yet neither obliged his choice. Could he really have preferred picking oakum to ruling a dinner table? He recognized that of the ignominious alternatives available to him, this was the least unheroic. (It was also the most modest.) Yeats was delighted when an old enemy of Wilde, perhaps Henley, met him in the street, and said with admiration of Wilde, 'He has made of infamy a new Thermopylae.' As for Yeats himself, he wrote later, 'I have never doubted, even for an instant, that he made the right decision, and that he owes to that decision half of his renown.' He submitted to the society he had criticized, and so earned the right to criticize it further.

Heroics were not the daily fare at the Leversons' house. Wilde did not claim heroism, nor do any more than resist pleas that he run away, without giving any grounds in particular, least of all grandiloquent ones. As the day of the trial approached, he showed something like resignation. He told Sherard that he thought he could bear a year's imprisonment, but Sherard warned him that he might well get the maximum sentence of two years. Wilde fell back for comfort on his love of Douglas, and wrote him letters of the most fervent kind: 'Now, in anguish and pain, in grief and humiliation, I feel that my love for you, your love for me, are the two signs of my life, the divine sentiments which make all bitterness bearable.' Douglas had admitted his own blame (he would deny it later) but Wilde said 'Let destiny, Nemesis, or the unjust gods alone receive the blame for everything that has happened.' And again, 'My sweet rose, my delicate flower,
 my lily of lilies, it is perhaps in prison that I am going

to test the power of love. I am going to see if I cannot make the bitter waters sweet by the intensity of the love I bear you.' These letters were of a different kind from those produced in court, which had been very nearly the formal literary productions that Wilde claimed. He was still prodigal of phrases: 'None of God's created beings, and you are the Morning Star to me, have been so wildly worshipped, so madly adored.' Beneath the purple alliteration was real feeling. Douglas wryly commented long afterwards in his *Autobiography*: 'The emotion of the great crisis fanned the waning fires of our devotion to each other.' He replied to Wilde with less eloquence, though with comparable emotion. He also wrote to his brother, begging him to make Wilde leave England while it was still possible. Percy replied that he hoped he would. In Paris Bosie took heart and wrote to Wilde, 'It seems too dreadful to be here without you, but I hope you will join me next week. Do keep up your spirits, my dearest darling. I continue to think of you day and night, and send you all my love. I am always your own loving and devoted boy Bosie.'

Douglas's state of mind in this period was exceedingly disturbed. He sent a series of letters to the press, of varying degrees of indiscretion. On 19 April he had written to the *Star* to complain of Wilde's being prejudged, and of Sir John Bridge's obvious bias against him. But the principal part of the letter read:

I feel, therefore, that I am taking my life in my hands in daring to raise my voice against the chorus of the pack of those who are now hounding Mr Oscar Wilde to his ruin; the more so as I feel assured that the public has made up its mind to accept them as it has accepted everybody and everything connected with this case, at Mr Carson's valuation. I, of course, am the undutiful son who, in his arrogance and folly, has kicked against his kind and affectionate father, and who has further aggravated his offence by not running away and hiding his face after the discomfiture of his friend.

Wilde understandably felt even at the time, though he did not tell Douglas till later, that this was a commonplace production; it was worse, indeed, because Douglas saw himself as the center of interest. He followed this up five days later with a letter saying he had received thousands of letters in support of his stand for Wilde. By 25 May the French press had caught up with him and Georges Docquois published an interview with him on that date. Douglas had claimed that he left England (on the second day of Wilde's trial, according to Raffalovich) because of the illness of his mother in Italy, but the press had found out she was in fact well. He now admitted that he had left because Wilde's lawyers had warned him he might be called as a witness, which he did not want. He had arrived in Paris on 15 May, but dodged the press for eight days. Asked about his letter to *Le Temps*, he explained, 'You do not know what an absolutely abominable man the Marquess of Queensberry is . . . Until I was twelve, I saw him at most twenty times, and I didn't feel at all sure from the way he treated me that I was his son.' The reporter inquired delicately about his relationship with Wilde, but Douglas insisted it was extraterrestrial, a communion together in the symbol rather than something seedy ('*louche*'). He knew no joy greater than to dine with Wilde when the latter was in 'good form.' They had once been joined by a dilettantish pleasure, now they were joined by persecution. To another French journalist he wrote on 30 May that he knew a hundred overt homosexuals in the best English society.

Lady Queensberry had some inkling of how Bosie was behaving, and she encouraged her son Percy to go to Rouen to see him at the end of May. She also consulted an old friend, the Reverend Sebastian Bowden, and asked him to find some trustworthy person to stay with Bosie and prevent his behaving foolishly out of loyalty to the fallen Wilde. Bowden asked More Adey to do this; Adey replied that his first duty was to Robert Ross, but that he would deal with Douglas as soon as he had calmed Ross down. Ross's family meanwhile forbade his remaining with Douglas, and Douglas, as Adey informed Bowden, planned a trip to Florence to see Lord Henry Somerset, almost as scandalous a character as Wilde.

A NEW THERMOPYLAE

How steep the stairs within kings' houses are.

Meanwhile Wilde was faced with the reality of his last trial. On its eve, 21 May, he serenely bade his friends farewell, and informed each of a little present from the few possessions left to him which would be a souvenir in case he did not return. When he was going to his room he asked Ada Leverson to leave a sleeping draught for him on the mantelpiece, not that he would take it, but that its presence would have a magical effect. Next day, before leaving with More Adey to join Stewart Headlam, he said to her, 'If the worst comes to the worst, Sphinx, you'll write to me?' During the next six days he was met in the morning and escorted back at night by Headlam, sometimes by Percy Douglas as well. At the Old Bailey all the seats were taken, so Queensberry, wearing a white cravat and a flower, had to stand, listening attentively, small and ferocious. Sir Edward Clarke was determined to try to secure some advantage for Wilde, and moved that Wilde and Taylor should be tried separately. Sir Frank Lockwood as Solicitor-General opposed the motion, on the grounds that the cases were intertwined. But Mr Justice Sir Alfred Wills ruled in Clarke's favor. Lockwood then proposed to take Taylor's case first, and Clarke again protested, for Taylor really had no defense at all, was well known to the police, and certain to be convicted. Over Clarke's protest the judge agreed. He said that Taylor had been in prison for seven weeks already, without bail, and that his trial should be delayed no longer.

This decision, which seemed minor, was very much to Wilde's detriment. The testimony in the Taylor case would involve him as well, and if Taylor were convicted, Wilde could scarcely be acquitted by the same jury without evident injustice. The Taylor case was quickly heard and quickly decided. The prosecutor had decided to reduce the charge from sodomy to indecency, as being easier to prove, and to secure a conviction. Taylor was found guilty on two counts of indecency with the Parker brothers, but not guilty of procuring Wood for Wilde, since, as the judge pointed out, he had not introduced the two men to each other. One of the Parker brothers had been promised immunity by ex-Inspector Littlefield if he would turn state's evidence against Wilde, but he nobly refused. Mr Justice Wills deferred sentence. Queensberry sent a telegram to his son Percy's wife: 'To Lady Douglas – must congratulate on verdict. Cannot on Percy appearance. Looked like a dug-up corpse. Fear too much madness in kissing. Taylor guilty. Wilde's turn to-morrow. Queensberry.' He also, on the mistaken notion that Wilde was staying with Percy and her, went to their house that night, knocked on the door, and made a disturbance. To Percy's wife he sent an illustration from a popular weekly of an iguanodon, with a childish note, 'Perhaps an ancestor of Oscar Wilde.' The following morning in Bond Street, in front of Scott's the hatters, Percy caught sight of his father and asked him if he were going to continue to annoy his wife with his communications. A street fight broke out, with Lord Douglas getting a black eye. They were both arrested and bound over next day on their own sureties of £500 to keep the peace for six months.

In this atmosphere of near-hysteria, the second trial of Oscar Wilde was to take place. The press had been discussing Wilde for weeks, with condemnation general except for *Reynolds's News*, which had private information about the extraordinary zeal with which Wilde was being prosecuted. Most of the newspapers considered that Queensberry had rightly brought down the 'High Priest of the Decadents,' as the *National Observer* saw fit to label Wilde.

The trial had few surprises. It became clear that two of the most important witnesses, the brothers Parker, were being maintained at Chiswick under the care of a Crown detective. It did not become clear, though it was apparently true, that all the witnesses had been receiving £5 a week from the beginning of Wilde's prosecution of Queensberry until his conviction. The star witness, Charles Parker, had received a new suit of clothes at Crown expense, ostensibly because he could not appear in court in a soldier's uniform. (He was to be cashiered.) This time the prosecution began not with him, however, but with Shelley, who made his usual blubbering denunciation of Wilde's sexual advances. This was again countered by the now familiar letters which he addressed to Wilde after the alleged offenses, asking for financial help. For a moment or two the case veered in Wilde's favor as the judge ruled that Shelley was, as Harris had claimed, an accomplice, and therefore not credible unless corroborated. This eliminated the prosecution's trump card, since Shelley alone of the important witnesses was neither male prostitute nor blackmailer. The next day Sir Frank Lockwood, once Wilde's friend, tried to persuade the judge to change his view, but the judge stood firm. Lockwood was heard to murmur outside, 'The old fool!' Testimony disclosed that the person who introduced Taylor to Wilde was Lockwood's nephew by marriage, Maurice Schwabe, a point upon which Lockwood was careful not to dilate.

Clarke did his best. He pointed out that, as anyone could see who had been at the other trials, Wilde was a broken man. It was inconceivable that he would have subjected himself to possible prosecution, by charging Queensberry with libel, if he had himself been so vulnerable. 'This trial seems to be operating as an act of indemnity for all the blackmailers in London,' he said, and it was obvious that the witnesses could better have been the accused rather than the accusers. They had

 nothing on Wilde, for otherwise they would have

blackmailed him relentlessly. Charles Parker was an uncorroborated witness, and a peculiarly unstable one. The testimony of the chambermaids did not prove that Wilde had committed any improper acts. 'If on an examination of the evidence you, therefore, feel it your duty to say that the charges against the prisoner have not been proved, then I am sure that you will be glad that the brilliant promise which has been clouded by these accusations, and the bright reputation which was so nearly quenched in the torrent of prejudice which a few weeks ago was sweeping through the press, have been saved by your verdict from absolute ruin; and that it leaves him, a distinguished man of letters and a brilliant Irishman, to live among us a life of honour and repute, and to give in the maturity of his genius gifts to our literature, of which he has given only the promise in his early youth.'

The last day of the trial, 25 May, was the Queen's birthday. In the midst of patriotic fervor Lockwood made his final speech for the prosecution. He raked Wilde over; he dealt with the suspect letters to Douglas, the payment of blackmail to Wood, the relations with Taylor, Wood, Parker, Conway, which he insisted corroborated each other. If the evidence of the chambermaids was false, why had not Lord Alfred

Douglas been called to deny it? As Wilde listened to 'Lockwood's appalling denunciation,' which sounded, he said later, 'like a thing out of Tacitus, like a passage in Dante, like one of Savonarola's indictments of the Popes at Rome,' he felt 'sickened with horror at what I heard. Suddenly it occurred to me, "*How splendid it would be, if I was saying all this about myself!*" I saw then at once that what is said of a man is nothing. The point is, who says it.' As he wrote to Ross later, 'the idea of "The Ballad of Reading Gaol" came to me while I was in the dock.' He was not cowed, his imagination was secretly triumphing over the proceedings.

Then came the summing-up. Mr Justice Wills was too prosaic to accept the affectation of Wilde's letters to Douglas as anything but indecent, and he spoke of them in unpleasant terms as Mr Justice Charles had not. As he went on he became more vehement, as if the heinousness of the offense was being borne in upon him the more he talked of it. 'It is the worst case I have ever tried,' he declared. He agreed that the fecal stains on the Savoy sheets might have been due to diarrhoea, but did not encourage this supposition. He impressed upon the jury the importance of maintaining the highest moral tone. The jury retired at half past three, and returned at twenty-five minutes to six with a question about some minor evidence. Lockwood, conscious that the rejection of Shelley's testimony meant that only the testimony of accomplices was left, said to Clarke, 'You'll dine your man in Paris tomorrow.' But Clarke said, 'No, no, no.' The jury retired again but returned a few minutes later to find the defendant guilty on all counts except that relating to Edward Shelley. Clarke asked the judge not to pass sentence until the next session, so as to consider a legal technicality. But the Solicitor-General opposed the motion, and the judge rejected it. He then turned to the prisoners:

Oscar Wilde and Alfred Taylor, the crime of which you have been convicted is so bad that one has to put stern restraint upon one's self to prevent one's self from describing, in language which I would rather not use, the sentiments which must rise to the breast of every man of honour who has heard the details of these two terrible trials. That the jury have arrived at a correct verdict in this case I cannot persuade myself to entertain the shadow of a doubt; and I hope, at all events that those who sometimes imagine that a judge is half-hearted in the cause of decency and morality because he takes care no prejudice shall enter into the case, may see that that is consistent at least with the common sense of indignation at the horrible charges brought home to both of you.

It is no use for me to address you. People who can do these things must be dead to all sense of shame, and one cannot hope to produce any effect upon them. It is the worst case I have ever tried. That you, Taylor, kept a kind of male brothel it is impossible to doubt. And that you, Wilde, have been the centre of a circle of extensive corruption of the most hideous kind among young men, it is equally impossible to doubt.

I shall, under such circumstances, be expected to pass the severest sentence that the law allows. In my judgement it is totally inadequate for such a case as this. The sentence of the Court is that each of you be imprisoned and kept to hard labour for two years.

A cry of 'Shame' was heard in the court. Wilde blanched and his discomposed face worked with pain. 'My God, my God!' he said. He struggled to speak, and may have managed to say (though witnesses differ), 'And I? May I say nothing, my lord?' But the judge merely waved his hand to the warders, who took hold of Wilde just as he swayed and seemed about to fall to the ground. Taylor followed him, indifferent, as if conscious of having no place in the drama. But he had shielded Wilde, as Wilde had shielded Douglas. (After serving his sentence Taylor emigrated to America and oblivion.) Outside, Yeats said, the harlots danced on the pavement. They were delighted to have this rival removed. Lord Queensberry, too, was triumphant, and that night he and Charles Brookfield and Charles Hawtrey held a victory dinner in celebration.

PENGUIN 60s

ISABEL ALLENDE · *Voices in My Ear*
NICHOLSON BAKER · *Playing Trombone*
LINDSEY BAREHAM · *The Little Book of Big Soups*
KAREN BLIXEN · *From the Ngong Hills*
DIRK BOGARDE · *Coming of Age*
ANTHONY BURGESS · *Childhood*
ANGELA CARTER · *Lizzie Borden*
CARLOS CASTANEDA · *The Sorcerer's Ring of Power*
ELIZABETH DAVID · *Peperonata and Other Italian Dishes*
RICHARD DAWKINS · *The Pocket Watchmaker*
GERALD DURRELL · *The Pageant of Fireflies*
RICHARD ELLMANN · *The Trial of Oscar Wilde*
EPICURUS · *Letter on Happiness*
MARIANNE FAITHFULL · *Year One*
KEITH FLOYD · *Hot and Spicy Floyd*
ALEXANDER FRATER · *Where the Dawn Comes Up Like Thunder*
ESTHER FREUD · *Meeting Bilal*
JOHN KENNETH GALBRAITH · *The Culture of Contentment*
ROB GRANT AND DOUG NAYLOR · *Scenes from the Dwarf*
ROBERT GRAVES · *The Gods of Olympus*
JANE GRIGSON · *Puddings*
SOPHIE GRIGSON · *From Sophie's Table*
KATHARINE HEPBURN · *Little Me*
SUSAN HILL · *The Badness Within Him*
ALAN HOLLINGHURST · *Adventures Underground*
BARRY HUMPHRIES · *Less is More Please*
HOWARD JACOBSON · *Expulsion from Paradise*
P. D. JAMES · *The Girl Who Loved Graveyards*
STEPHEN KING · *Umney's Last Case*
LAO TZU · *Tao Te Ching*
DAVID LEAVITT · *Chips Is Here*

PENGUIN 60s

LAURIE LEE · *To War in Spain*
PATRICK LEIGH FERMOR · *Loose as the Wind*
ELMORE LEONARD · *Trouble at Rindo's Station*
DAVID LODGE · *Surprised by Summer*
BERNARD MAC LAVERTY · *The Miraculous Candidate*
SHENA MACKAY · *Cloud-Cuckoo-Land*
NORMAN MAILER · *The Dressing Room*
PETER MAYLE · *Postcards from Summer*
JAN MORRIS · *Scenes from Havian Life*
BLAKE MORRISON · *Camp Cuba*
VLADIMIR NABOKOV · *Now Remember*
REDMOND O'HANLON · *A River in Borneo*
STEVEN PINKER · *Thinking in Tongues*
CRAIG RAINE · *Private View*
CLAUDIA RODEN · *Ful Medames and Other Vegetarian Dishes*
HELGE RUBINSTEIN · *Chocolate Parfait*
SIMON SCHAMA · *The Taking of the Bastille*
WILL SELF · *The Rock of Crack As Big As the Ritz*
MARK SHAND · *Elephant Tales*
NIGEL SLATER · *30-Minute Suppers*
RICK STEIN · *Fresh from the Sea*
LYTTON STRACHEY · *Florence Nightingale*
PAUL THEROUX · *Slow Trains to Simla*
COLIN THUBRON · *Samarkand*
MARK TULLY · *Beyond Purdah*
LAURENS VAN DER POST · *Merry Christmas, Mr Lawrence*
MARGARET VISSER · *More than Meets the Eye*
GAVIN YOUNG · *Something of Samoa*

and

Thirty Obituaries from Wisden · SELECTED BY MATTHEW ENGEL